Don't Be Hasty with Science Safety!

Bridget Pederson

Consulting Editors, Diane Craig, M.A./Reading Specialist
and Susan Kosel, M.A. Education

ABDO
Publishing Company

Published by ABDO Publishing Company, 4940 Viking Drive, Edina, Minnesota 55435.

Printed in the United States.

Credits
Edited by: Pam Price
Curriculum Coordinator: Nancy Tuminelly
Cover and Interior Design and Production: Mighty Media
Photo Credits: AbleStock, BananaStock Ltd., Corbis Images, Creatas, Digital Vision, Photodisc, ShutterStock, Wewerka Photography

Library of Congress Cataloging-in-Publication Data

Pederson, Bridget.
    Don't be hasty with science safety! / Bridget Pederson.
        p. cm. -- (Science made simple)
    ISBN 10 1-59928-580-0 (hardcover)
    ISBN 10 1-59928-581-9 (paperback)

    ISBN 13 978-1-59928-580-1 (hardcover)
    ISBN 13 978-1-59928-581-8 (paperback)
    1. Science rooms and equipment--United States--Safety measures--Juvenile literature.
  2. Science--Experiments--Juvenile literature. I. Title.

Q183.3.A1.P419 2007
507.8--dc22   2006021169

SandCastle Level: Transitional

SandCastle™ books are created by a professional team of educators, reading specialists, and content developers around five essential components—phonemic awareness, phonics, vocabulary, text comprehension, and fluency—to assist young readers as they develop reading skills and strategies and increase their general knowledge. All books are written, reviewed, and leveled for guided reading, early reading intervention, and Accelerated Reader® programs for use in shared, guided, and independent reading and writing activities to support a balanced approach to literacy instruction. The SandCastle™ series has four levels that correspond to early literacy development. The levels help teachers and parents select appropriate books for young readers.

Emerging Readers
(no flags)

Beginning Readers
(1 flag)

Transitional Readers
(2 flags)

Fluent Readers
(3 flags)

These levels are meant only as a guide. All levels are subject to change.

Safety is very important. Scientists need to be neat and organized and do experiments with caution. There are many safety rules when working in the lab.

Words used to talk about safety:
accident
careful
dangerous
experiment
goggles
organize

 protect your eyes from harmful chemicals.

It is important to be careful when handling sharp objects such as ✂.

Always wash your after working in the science lab.

Glass objects, such as , can break and should be handled with care.

When working with chemicals, don't touch your 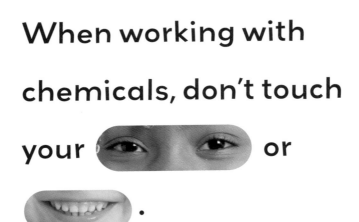 or .

Wear an to protect your clothes from spills.

Don't Be Hasty with Science Safety!

Science Safety:
- use the right tool
- wear goggles
- wear an apron

Emma likes to experiment. She is careful to avoid an accident.

I am careful to use the right tool. It's just like the teacher showed me in school.

It's important for Emma to organize. She also wears goggles to protect her eyes.

Mixing chemicals can be fun, but you must be safe until you are done.

14

Emma wears an apron over her dress. That way she won't end up a mess.

Many experiments can cause a splash. Protect your clothes so they don't end up in the trash.

Safety Every Day!

Zach asks his teacher for help when he works on a hard experiment.

By asking questions, you can avoid accidents and stay safe.

Felix doesn't drink the liquid from his experiment because it may be dangerous.

Felix knows it is not safe to eat or drink anything used in a science experiment.

Ginny listens carefully while her teacher explains the directions for the experiment.

Listening to directions before starting an experiment helps avoid accidents and keeps you safe.

Joan and Victor know it is important to work slowly and carefully to prevent accidents in the science lab.

How do you stay safe in science class?

Glossary

apron – garment worn over the clothes to protect against spills.

chemical – a substance made or used in a science experiment.

goggles – large glasses worn over the eyes to protect them.

hasty – done too fast to be safe or wise about what you are doing.

test tube – a glass tube used in experiments.